CW01315073

www.clivecreative.com

Copyright ©2021 Clive Austin

All Rights Reserved

ISBN: 978-1-291-09517-3

This book does not replace the advice of a medical professional, be they biological or psychological. Consult your physician or health care professional before making any changes to your diet, lifestyle or regular health plan.

The information in this book was correct at the time of publication, but the Author does not assume any liability for loss or damage caused by errors or omissions.

While parts of the text contained within this book may require digesting the author accepts no responsibility for persons who take metaphor and allegory literally and physically try to eat this book.

LIVE CREATIVE

BOOK ONE

THE PATH

CREATING YOUR LIFE &
LETTING LIFE CREATE YOU

CLIVE AUSTIN
www.clivecreative.com

All of this is
provisional.

I have just
made it up.

Once you understand this
you will better understand
the nature of the path.

INDEX

	FORWARD	11
ONE	CREATIVITY	13
TWO	THE COSMOS	25
THREE	BE YOURSELF	33
FOUR	DOING WHAT YOU LOVE & DOING WHAT NEEDS TO BE DONE	43
FIVE	WITHOUT FEAR OF FAILURE OR DESIRE FOR SUCCESS	47
SIX	MAKING THE UNFAMILIAR FAMILIAR	49
SEVEN	INTIMACY	53
EIGHT	THE BALANCE OF OPPOSITES	57
NINE	DON'T LET THE BASTARDS GET YOU DOWN	61
TEN	BREAK THE RULES	65
ELEVEN	MAKE NEW RULES	67
TWELVE	THERE IS NO TWELVE	73

FORWARD

The purpose of this book is to help you make more of life,
to help you make more of *your* life.

It is about your relationship to,
and with,
life.

Most of all to the creative essence that life is:
As it manifests around you,
As it manifests within you,
and,
As you manifest it:
Through your thoughts,
Through your words,
and through your actions.

This creative essence fuels your capacity to adapt, to solve problems, to invent solutions, to change yourself, and to change the world, or at least bits of it.

It is everywhere and it is everything.

Including you.

ONE

CREATIVITY

Let us begin at the beginning.

Creativity is the quality of bringing something into existence that wasn't there before.

This process and its effects are everywhere.

Galaxies, trees, portraits, ice cream, computers, the nameless thing in the shed, cake, trousers, elephants, skirting board, missiles, fridges, statues, play parks, rulers, paperclips, skyscrapers, toffee, albatrosses....

It's an endless list.

You are on it too.

Creativity appears to be what the universe is, and while there are destructive forces too, and while it can be difficult to discern between which is which and what is when and where, the taking apart of things and the putting together of them appear to be two sides of the same coin.

As far as this text goes I would like to propose, for the sake of fluidity and simplicity, that when using the term creative this paradox is implied, and more than this, that when using the term creative I am pointing to something positive, something generative. Something that adds to life.

Anyway, back to the list.

Not only are you on the list as something that was created within this universe, but also, you are a part of it, and not only are you a part of it, you are creating it to.

You are the creative universe.

With limitations.

Your conscious awareness and your agency can be applied to make of *it*, and of yourself, all that you are willing and capable of making.

A part of the universe creating itself.

Your ideas, inspirations, and insights, are all embarkation points for potential creative quests and endeavours.

The limits of these quests and endeavours are yours to discover. That there will be boundaries you had not considered may well be true. That you are capable of exceeding boundaries that you have put in place for yourself I can almost guarantee.

The truth is.... well, we'll get to that bit.

This all sounds very romantic I know, almost limitless possibility and potential restricted only by your own capacity to imagine alternatives and let go of the identities that keep you feeling safe.

Is it really that simple?

Well, the idea is certainly simple enough. As for putting it into practice that would be a matter for you to find out.

Only you know that.

That it is possible. That bit I am quite happy to state.
Either way the fact remains. You have the power to create.

It is a magic power of sorts, one that many appear to have forgotten they have, or have been taught they do not need. Maybe you are, or have been, one of them.

You may even have thought that you could continue on through life believing that creativity was the reserve of artists, musicians, chefs, architects, journalists, and certain types of artisan sandwich makers; any of the occupations that fit within the margins defined by the prevailing cultures to which such roles belong.

Such people, when asked if they are creative will often tell you that they are not.

Some will say they wish they were.

The truth is, barring rare neurological diversities, we are all creative and to a greater or lesser extent we continue with this potential until our end.

It is not unlike a muscle.
Some people have just forgotten how to use it.

Sadly, for those who do not question further, the value and the potential of their own creativity to enrich their lives remains hidden, out of view, lingering on the periphery of memory, at the back of kitchen draws, or tucked away in boxes in the shadows of attics and dusty garage shelves.

For those who are curious, for those eager or already using creativity to enhance their lives, I would like to suggest that there are two types.

For the sake of clarity and simplicity I would like you to consider the idea that creativity can occupy anywhere along a line between two ends of a spectrum.

At one end creativity is a conscious act.

at the other,

$\hspace{6cm}$ an unconscious one.

The first is a considered, designed, and focused act. It can involve analysis and planning and requires conscious cognition, often of parts and the order in which they need to be arranged.

The second flows into the world at its own rate and pace, and it is all you can do to capture it before it slips through the net of your imagination. Often it arrives in an ethereal state of completion and it is all the witness can do but capture it.

Conscious Creativity

At the consciously created end of the spectrum it is the choice of the individual to create something. It is considered. In this sense this type of creativity could be called conscious design. You think and act in alignment with your will, actively making choices and decisions based on reasoning and conscious aesthetic preferences. Perhaps it is more studious than playful, although not necessarily. Perhaps it is more of a science than an art. Again, perhaps not. Perhaps it is both. Either way, it is considered.

It is questioning how things or moments might be placed next to, on top of, inside of, beneath, at right angles to one another. How they might be balanced upon, merged with, taken apart, rebuilt, multiplied by, subtracted from, purified, distilled, painted blue, framed in gold, fired into the heavens, whatever your beautiful imagination can conjure.

It is about playing with material and the intervals between things, be they in time or space.

Meaning, colour, tone, proportion, volume, scale, pace, context of placement, there are so many variables, so many options. How one choses is where the creativity lies.

It has something to do with experience.

In music it is the intervals between notes that produce the melody and the rhythm. In sculpture it is the space *that is not the form* which defines what remains. The same is as true for painting, writing, and film as well.

There are rules to composition. They can be learnt, and they can be broken.

It is as much the gaps between things as it is about the things themselves.

Balance, harmony, composition, proportion, scale: conscious creation anticipates these variables and acts to influence and manipulate them. It is about being aware of what you are creating and/or how you are creating it *before* it is created.

It is the design and the crafting of a thing.

Unconscious Creativity

By contrast, unconscious creativity,
put simply,
comes from a place we are not conscious of.

It arrives as insight, inspiration, impression,
and/or an intuition.

Bear in mind that these moments of unconscious creativity can arise out of, or alongside, moments of conscious creativity too, and vice versa. They are not mutually exclusive states, but intertwine each other. As stated before, these are the conceptual ends of a spectrum rather than distinct and opposite modes of operating, even if sometimes it can appear that way. Which sometimes it can.

Also, they can operate as a continuum, with one feeding the other in a delicate, or even aggressive, or assertive flow - or even as conflict and tension.

Unconscious creativity can arrive without warning.
Sometimes at the most inappropriate moments.

If you know these moments, which I suspect many of you will, you will know that the challenge can be in how you channel or capture your insight into some recognisable, material form.

In such moments it can feel like you are in service to the ideas.

It is not uncommon for such things to be birthed in the depths of night, to sprout forth from that bardic state between waking and sleeping when the temptation to ignore its quiet voice in favour of dreaming sleep can be all too great.

And here is the first invitation:

To respect that quiet voice,
the inner sight that comes as inspiration.

Respond to it.

Form a relationship with it.

It is just a deeper part of you, the part from whose deeps the mystery of being emerges, sometimes in delicate and tentative steps and at other in a passionate flood.

Catching it,
affording it value,
showing gratitude for it,

all this signals to the unconscious that you value its gifts - the insights and the inspiration it is offering.

When you show it respect in this way it will often offer you more.

When you ignore it
it can fall silent.

It is not uncommon when building a bridge to the worlds within that you invite into your life a quality - something akin to an ally in yourself - a silent partner whose wisdom and insight is (at times) far in excess of what your conscious mind may even conceive possible, at least at first.

Of course, these are just aspects of you of which you are becoming conscious.

You are making friends with your mystery within.

Between wake and sleep is not the only time such offerings can emerge. Often spaces and times where we are tuned to let go of the pressures of the day will invite such states. Not least after carrying moments of tension: walks in nature, day dreams, train journeys, showers and baths, the bed of a lover. Even repetitive and mundane work can play a part. It is not uncommon to find inspiration in the moment we have planned to be somewhere else, somewhere important, sometime urgent.

There are no hard and fast rules but the muse does appear to appreciate the irony of sacrifice at least.

The question is, are you prepared to answer the call and act in the moment when inspiration arrives?

While your devotion will doubtless be rewarded, it invariably seems to come at a cost - at least until such time as that relationship develops, and your priorities shift - if indeed they do at all.

The point being, that they can.

This essence is not confined to the creation of *things,* or to framed events either, but is just as applicable to how you might choose to live life in a broader sense as well.

In so far as you can *consciously* create a path to follow through life in how you plan to live, you can also allow your *unconscious* to guide you by listening to the signals that it offers in each moment.

Living well appears to accommodate a blend of both.

TWO

THE COSMOS

As far as you might want to be more creative, or to allow the creative in you to show up more in your life, I'd like to invite you to read the following paragraphs quite closely, and to consider the implications of the ideas therein. We have touched on them already but there is a point to stating them again.

You are not separate from the universe you perceive around you. In this sense you are the universe perceiving itself.

You and it are made of the same substance; the same essence. You and it, and all of the other things that it appears to be, are just the same thing organised in different ways. Distinct patterns of atoms and molecules forming systems of larger things that just make everything *appear* separate.

This separation is valid and meaningful from any perspective that can perceive it. This means that you can avoid standing on spiky things when you have forgotten your shoes, get hugs from soft warm furry things, and ingest the shapes that are both tasty and nutritious.

It is equally valid to say that, at another level, everything is all the same thing. After all, that is what universe means - it is the everything that is, the biggest whole of which all things are part.

Within this universe of things, things form and things fall apart. In and of themselves these states are neither good nor bad, they just are. What makes them good or bad, positive or negative is your perspective, your experience, and your judgement.

Either way, because you are a part of the universe, you have the ability to create and destroy within you.

How you choose to use them is for you to decide, but have them you do, and use them you do, whether you have recognised it yet or not.

In these terms you are the universe creating itself.

Your choice and agency to create what you will is limited only by your form and nature. Your imagination, your influence, your conscience, your circumstance - such things define the edges of your potentials. While there are those who would argue that this is all just an illusion, it is a persistent enough one to continue acting as if it were true.

With these potentials you are free to create whatever you wish, in and of and out of yourself, and in, and of, and with, the world. As is everyone else, be it by themselves or in collaboration.

The world in which you live is, to a greater or lesser extent, the result of this process.

As are you.

Well, that's the theory.

Like I say, this is all made up.

It'll be down to you, or up to you (whichever perspective you prefer to take) as to how to make sense and use of it.

For the time being though, let's assume that the proposition is valid enough to play around with: that everything around you is a product of a creative universe, including you, and that you are, therefore, the universe creating itself.

The atoms that form the molecules that form the cells that form the organs and the limbs and the whole of you have been, and are being, endlessly recycled according to maps set out in your DNA and their (and your) adaptability to the environments you find yourself in.

Your potential is contained in this, within the limits of that code, and within your ability to adapt.

For example. Imagine two or three different locations you would like to live. For the sake of this exercise try to imagine extremes so that you get a clear sense of how the difference between the environments would cause you to adapt differently to each.

Maybe one is mountainous, another a city, another a foreign country, a beach, a jungle, a suburban housing estate, a war zone.

Each would elicit a different set of potentials, because to survive and prosper in each you would require different skills, you would acquire different knowledge. You would be a different version of yourself in each, because each would elicit the need for a different response. Yes, there would be a part of you that remained you, that wouldn't change. An oak is an oak and an ash is an ash, but they grow differently according to where they are planted. They must adapt to their environments in order to survive. As must you. The difference being that you can relocate yourself.

While there is something of you that you can anticipate would remain the same, there is also a sense that living in different environments, with different people, that these things would change you in some way.

The question is, how willing are you to be changed?

When you have no choice over your environments, or when you feel you have no choice over how you respond to them, then such situations can feel like an imposition in life.

Being at the effectual end of a situation can be frustrating, or depressing. For the most part people feel better when they feel like they are a cause in their world. At least I believe that will be true for those reading this book.

Having the choice to act, or claiming the choice to act, can be life changing, not least because you claim responsibility for your well being - or as much of it as you can. In the same way that power comes with responsibility, taking responsibility gives you a power because it returns a sense of control back to your life. While it is foolish to assume that such control is paramount, it is valuable.

Of course such change can require great effort and a courage to face certain truths. To leave behind what you have grown to believe you are and to meet the potential of who you might become, and then to live it, can leave you feeling vulnerable, bewildered, and confused. At least at the outset.

The degree to which each individual has the potential to create this change in their life will depend on a number of factors.

That they can though, I believe, is certain.

Whether or not you will, or even need to, will be a matter for your own consideration.

In a very real sense, the creative process that governs everything is in us - it *is* us, because we are not separate from the universe that is in essence creative. You are *it*, and therefore, you are *it* evolving - a part of its unfolding and its becoming.

Its creative becoming *is* what you are.

The more you are conscious of this, the more potential you have of tapping into it. You can create yourself and (to some significant degree) your world. Along with everyone and everything else you are the universe creating itself.

If you choose to view your life through this lens you will see that not only do you have a right to be creative, being creative is what you are already doing.

> You are an agency of a creative universe incarnated into a physical form that can manipulate and channel thoughts and matter into ideas and things.

If being creative is what you are already doing, whether you are aware of it or not, then it is fair to assume that you are doing one (or both) of two things. Either you are creating out of yourself, from your own conscious design - or your unconscious inspirations - or you are using your life to help manifest something inspired by another.

Every thought and every act is a contribution in this regard.

Either way, your actions are always helping to maintain or create something.

Being creative is a universal condition because it is the primary condition of the Universe.

So, because you are the universe, if your wish is to live more creatively, or to live with more creativity, you just have to be yourself.

THREE

BE YOURSELF

Whether or not you buy into the notion that you are a conscious part of a creative universe that is perceiving itself, it appears to be of benefit to be yourself within it.

Knowing what that means - to be yourself - requires that you know yourself - and knowing yourself requires that you recognise what it means to be alive - to live as the unique person that you are.

One begets the other, and so on, and so on. It's a cycle. You get up, you shower, you eat breakfast, you go somewhere, then you go somewhere else, maybe you speak to people, you do some more stuff, you return to the place where you sleep, you eat, maybe you have sex, maybe you go for a walk, maybe you sit in a chair and look at changing patterns of light, then you go to bed, maybe you sleep.

The better you get to know yourself the better you get at knowing what it means to be yourself - to be who you are. The more you show up to finding out why you do the things that you do, the more honest you are with yourself, the more you act in alignment with that version of yourself, the more authentic you become and the more knowledge you gain.

You get up, you shower, you eat breakfast, you go somewhere, then you go somewhere else, maybe you speak to people, you do some more stuff, you return to the place where you sleep, you eat, maybe you have sex, maybe you go for a walk, maybe you sit in a chair and look at changing patterns of light, then you go to bed, maybe you sleep, and you know why you did all of that. You know why you chose to do all of that, and you know that the bits you did not choose were chosen for you by your instincts. Either way, you know, and the knowing will inform whether you do the same thing tomorrow or not.

It all begins and ends with awareness.

Being with one's thoughts, emotions, feelings, intuitions and actions, from one moment to the next, is key in the process of developing this awareness of ourselves.

Accepting, allowing, and changing these qualities and conditions where they can be changed, and knowing when they can't, is all part of it.

The sense of authenticity that dwells in the moment of your being, the truth of the sensation *that is your experience* of being alive - from moment to moment to moment and on - this is the knowing and the being of yourself to which I speak.

It is not something that you find and then become.
It is something you recognise you are.
It is the process of you being and becoming.

Adaptation to your environment, to changes in it, and to changes in yourself, is essential for navigating the shifting topography of life.

The primary system of feedback in this is how you feel, is your emotional state.

You discover what feels good and what feels bad, what feels right and what feels wrong.

You discovered this as you grew. The shape of the world, its rough and its smooth edges, its hot plates, its fast traffic, its cool breezes on summer days. Within these spaces, with your process of discovery and becoming, you found the edges of who you are and what you were capable of. Each environment encountered and explored along the way afforded new insights into your potential.

Your attitude to these environments, and to yourself, affect how you meet the world.

It still does.

Discover what is beyond and what is inside.

In this way you deepen your knowledge of yourself.

In this way you *be* yourself, in all of your radical incompleteness.

In discovering more about yourself you come to learn what your intrinsic motivations are. You learn to recognise what is good and right for *you,* and for the world, and for those people whose lives intermingle with your own.

The path to knowing and being yourself is not always easy though. It requires courage - to live and to speak freely the truth within you.

Often, we are raised in environments where other people's expectations are impressed upon us. In the language of alchemy this is termed the prevailing spirit - you could call it conditioning or influence and get the same result.

When asked or pressured to conform, your essential spirit - or, if you prefer, your authentic self - gets compromised.

It steps back, steps away. Your adaptation gets steered from the outside.

Your "I don't do that sort of thing" is the result of a "We don't do that sort of thing" rather than an "I have chosen not to do that sort of thing because I have found it to be wrong, deleterious, or detrimental to do so."

The instinctual sense of 'knowing' what is best for you gets placed to the back of the queue in favour of a need that is imposed or delivered from outside your experience and your judgement.

Not to conform can mean expulsion or separation from the group, and expulsion or separation from the group can equal death, at least at an instinctual level. We are social beings after all. Such propositions can be frightening, in some cases terrifying because they can change your orientation to the world.

In your attempts to become what you feel you need to be in order to survive, you can become isolated from a way of being in the world that is actually more natural for you, more aligned to who and what you feel yourself to be. You compromise yourself, your true nature - your essential spirit.

The more you live true to *your* experience - the more you live by this sense of what you discover to be true within yourself, the more of a challenge it can be to others who want you to be more like them, or more like the you you once were. They want you to remain familiar and predictable. It just feels safer for them that way.

Some people, rather than face the effort required in confronting their own nature and realising what life asks of them, prefer to live according to collective beliefs and rules that maintain comfort and security for the group.

It is not that this is wrong, it is more a question of where and how and when and for whom that is an optimal way to live. It is for each individual to make their own judgement this.

As long as certain rights and liberties don't get lost in the process of relinquishing personal responsibility then is it really that bad?

Creativity in life appears to require that you take charge of your actions and your agency in the world. Living creatively often challenges conformity because conformity, by its nature, asks you to follow an established path and not to create our own. Creativity, because it is the bringing into existence of something that was not there before, messes with that.

Being yourself then is about finding, or creating, the path that is yours, that is right for you. This path may be an established one, but even if it is, you can be sure that if you are choosing to follow it it is because it is the right one for you. You are choosing it with awareness - at least as much as you can bring. You know why you are following the path because you know who you are and what you want. Or the path is leading you to discover a greater level of awareness of yourself by following it.

You are not following it because that is what is expected of you, or because you are fearful of what might happen to you if you don't, or because you don't believe that you could live any other way.

You are following your path because you can, because you choose to do so, because you need to do so, and because it feels right and/or it feels good.

Do not be fooled though.

Honesty and authenticity require that you confront yourself. This process can uncover old beliefs, assumptions, and patterns of behaviour that do not, or have not been serving you. Some of them may still be attached to versions of yourself that were assembled in the past and are, at some level, still holding on to it.

The degree to which you can recognise these patterns and behaviours and relinquish them will be the degree to which you can transform away from them. If you wish to move on with the acceptance of who you are in the present, unencumbered by the emotional residue of the past, then I recommend it.

One of the greatest causes of emotional pain in life can be derived from holding onto versions of yourself that you are no longer capable of either being or becoming.

If you have identified your survival or well being with a fixed version of yourself, a 'you' that you feel like you *need* to be or become in order to survive or prosper then you may well have built yourself a trap.

Whether this idea of yourself is of your own construction or the result of another's influence upon you makes little difference. Letting go of it can sometimes take monumental effort as it can feel like a part of you is dying, or that you will die if you do. This is because the idea of you as that thing will.

If running a kitten sanctuary in Peru is really what you are all about the more power to you, but if it is a construct, an idea of what or who you think you should be in order to gain love or a sense of worth or self esteem, then let it go.

There is a more whole version of yourself waiting on the other side with a range of potential just waiting to be discovered and activated.

At other times these constructs, these frames of identity are comfortable enough just to slip out of existence, because the potential future that is on offer is just so much better.

> You must die to yourself in order to be reborn as the person you were meant to become.

This metaphorical motif pervades myth and legend across cultures and millennia.

For good reason.

The sense of losing what we know of our identity can feel frightening, but what lies on the other side is a version of us that is more than we could even believe possible before.

A word of warning though.

Before you go pulling yourself apart make sure that you practice standing in yourself for a while. What I mean by this is simple. Find the things that you are certain about in yourself - those parts of your nature that do not change or shift in a storm. Get used to standing in that place and only go at the pace that is right for you to do so. If in doubt do what you love, do what feels right, and do what needs to be done.

FOUR

DOING WHAT YOU LOVE & DOING WHAT NEEDS TO BE DONE

This is about energy.

Not doing what you love drains the energy from your body.

Not doing what needs to be done drains energy from your thoughts.

When you do something that you love your life force has a tendency to flow in that direction because the act of doing it has enough meaning, value, or joy that it is a reward in and of itself.

You love the process or the end result so much that you can work ceaselessly and tirelessly towards it.

While you may tire from the physical or mental labour of it what is depleted can be regained with rest. It is a natural tiredness that is the result of effort.

That is how love works.

You don't question it.

You just feel it and it moves you to act.

Life also calls you to do what needs to be done.

The more time you spend thinking about these tasks the more energy you direct away from doing other things. The thought of the task becomes the task. Meanwhile the dishes done get done, the bin stays full, tax returns unfilled, lawns overgrown, cars unwashed.

Certainly you can love, or even learn to love the tasks that *need* to be done, but that is not always the case. Your survival may require that you act at times, or in ways, that you would prefer not to.

When you act on what needs to be done *when* it needs to be done then there is a tendency to use your energy far more effectively, because it doesn't have time to get used up in thinking about doing the task.

Certainly there is a fine line. Not all thought about a task is bad. Some degree of planning can be essential, but I bet you know someone who researches projects to death and never actually acts towards their completion. There will be many reasons why someone can end up this way, but the upshot is, if research, planning, and rumination becomes inaction then what purpose does it really serve?

The point of this chapter is about identifying how you are using your energy because your energy, your life force and how you use it is a valuable part of the puzzle.

Of course, if you can find a way of doing what you love *and* doing what needs to be done then you will most likely have discovered the answer to one of the greatest riddles of life.

"How shall I live?"

FIVE

WITHOUT FEAR OF FAILURE OR DESIRE FOR SUCCESS

When you do something without fear of failure or desire for success you free yourself from expectation.

When something is created free of expectation it seems to have a life of its own, a certain purity and freedom.

There is no reason for it to be anything other than it is.

While there may well be plans to be followed, without an emotional attachment to an outcome, the shaping of things is guided by a quality that seems freer in its expression somehow.

When you can engage in life in this way there is a sort of magic that appears to happen. It has something to do with relaxing away from outcome and engaging those parts of yourself that can be more playful, because you are naturally more at ease.

You may or may not know this but apex predators, when they hunt, activate the exact same circuits in their brains as when they play. They are not stressed, and while they may tire, their motivation to seek and play pushes them to continue on once rested.

It is this sense of play that helps form solutions to problems. If you have ever lost your sense of play you might find that it was because you became invested in an outcome.

Non attachment, non disinterest.

This attitude can make a great ally.

SIX

MAKING THE UNFAMILIAR FAMILIAR

Life can be unpredictable.

You know this.

You don't need me to give you examples.

As a result people have evolved with a biological hardwiring to be wary of things they are unfamiliar with, especially things that appear difficult to predict.

Fear of the unknown is not unfounded either.

You spot difference for a reason and cannot always know if something or someone is a threat until you get to know the true edges. Even then, depending on past experience, it may take a while for the accuracy of your measure to set in.

Making the unfamiliar familiar is not about staring into the mouth of the lion, it is not even about edging towards him from a safe distance with a high powered telescope and an escape plan. The point is not about putting yourself in danger, but rather, learning that not all situations that are unpredictable or unfamiliar are as dangerous as you might imagine at first glance.

Perhaps this is not you anyway, in which case, feel free to skip this chapter.

For others, knowing the limits of things can take some getting used to.

Learning to live with the discomfort of *not knowing* enough, or not knowing clearly - of uncertainty - and still *acting* in the world can feel like a difficult path to tread because fear and trepidation kill playfulness and if you wish to encourage creativity and the creative into your life then learning more ways to be at ease in the world is fundamental.

No one wants to be stressed out facing uncertainty and the anxiety that can accompany it but, by the same token, there can be as much anxiety and stress caused from living in a place in which you feel stuck.

Not facing up to challenges, be they new experiences, new people, or new places, can be equally frustrating. When deep down you have a sense that you have more potential than is currently being realised where else can you go with this?

Making the unfamiliar familiar is not just about learning how to live in uncomfortable places either. It is recognising that uncomfortable places are not always as dangerous as our biological anticipation or social conditioning around them might have led us to believe.

Whilst moments of great ingenuity can arise out of extremes (necessity is, as they say, the mother of invention) I am not suggesting that you throw yourself into situations that push you to extremes *unless* you feel ready to do so.

It's one thing to swim with dolphins, another to swim with sharks.

How far you will want to push your own particular envelope will depend upon where you are on your own particular path.

The more familiar you can be with unfamiliarity the better prepared you will be for engaging with the world in a way that enables you to meet more of it.

Less fear, more intimacy.

The questions of why or what might have caused you to feel unsafe in the first place can be irrelevant. It is often more important to discover what helps you feel safe or courageous *now*, in the moment you are in.

SEVEN

INTIMACY

Intimacy is not familiarity.

Intimacy can be an invitation to embrace each experience with the same explorative delight of not knowing the fullness of the experience that awaits you.

A willingness to dive into the depths, to soak oneself in the unknown. The willingness to discover.

It is also about knowing.

If creation is about placing things then the more examples of things you have to draw on, the broader base you will have when creating, be that consciously and unconsciously.

If you wish to grow and learn the craft behind your art then living closer to your tools and your materials will do that.

If you wish to develop your art then live closer to the world.

To grow your soul swim in deeper waters.

The edges of the boundaries you encounter envelope the experience of your life. To grow you must test them, stretch them, maybe even tear them if you must.

On the inside is all that is familiar, beyond them the prospect of both adventure and misadventure.

Intimacy gives you the knowledge of life and of its material. You learn how well material will stretch over a frame. How far you can push a structure up into the sky. How two colours will look when mixed. How two or more notes will sound when played together. How your body will, can, might move through space.

Developing this knowledge requires a willingness to see things for what they are and not what you want them to be. And a willingness to discover what they are beyond both. It is to listen to the stories of things, to see the brash exterior and at the same time hear the quieter currents that flow beneath the surface of things, and vice versa.

There is the tender and the robust. Intimacy is knowing which is which. When to hold on lightly and allow the wings to unfurl and fly, and when to grasp firmly enough not to let them fail or fall.

Intimacy is knowing how and when to walk on ice.
To watch pollen dance on breezes in the evening sun.
It is to know the contents of another's wardrobe.
To know how much seasoning to add to a soup.
It is to know the ocean well enough to navigate by the waves alone.

Intimacy requires that you approach yourself in the same way. To know what you *can* know, and to know what you cannot, and to know that knowing the edges of both requires that you surrender to the experience of being at the deepest levels that you can.

Souls seek parts of themselves.
Some that have remained previously unmet, undiscovered, or even lost. These meetings can be as meaningful for the part sought as the part seeking.

It can happen in a way that one or both are moved to a state of being that transcends the commonality of the everyday. Something touches them. Something reaches a part that normal life cannot.

The depth becomes as recognisable as the surface. You are moved, often in ineffable ways.

It is an attempt to share and discover more of the mystery within.

Intimacy will reveal more creativity, and creativity will express an intimacy with life.

EIGHT

THE BALANCE OF OPPOSITES

One way to look at creativity is as the balancing of opposites, as the regulation within a system between two extremes. This is the idea that creativity is a homeostatic function.

Systems function on the exchange of information between parts and those parts have their own fields of operation that differ by varying degree. Fluctuations occur in the exchange of information both within and between those parts. Each has limits to what it can perceive and process. As a reflexive function creativity can be seen as an attempt to make sure that information exchange is somehow optimised towards growth and adaptation.

The egg is an adaptation that contains and protects the growth of life within it.

A bird creates a nest as a place to hatch and protect its young from the elements, to contain them safely until it is time for them to fly.

The tree that holds the nest is the result of an adaptation to the soil in which its sapling roots first reached, and into the sky that helped it grow.

All are the products of environmental adaptations.

Each in turn is a complex sequence of reactions to the formation of the continents on which they grew.

All on a planet whose aggregation of matter was rolled into being over millennia in the orbit of a mighty sun.

While those of us still fortunate to do so struggle on some days to decide what to have for lunch.

Artists, whose perceptions and adaptations urge them to create artefacts and events that challenge convention and/or elicit emotion are no different.

Anyone or anything that is driven to redress a perceived imbalance, be it as a conscious act or through some emotional drive resulting from an unconscious impulse, fits in with this frame.

There are some who propose that if you knew all the laws of the universe and all of the starting positions of all of the parts that it contains, then you would be able to plot the trajectories of all things; marbles, lightbulbs, the decaying orbits of distant planets, every combination of sandwich filling, and the shapes of people's lives - not least your own.

You would be able to predict, without fail, every event before it even happened, every thing prior to it coming into existence.

The universe would be, in your eyes, a very ordered place.

Life might also be a bit dull as a result but there you go, you can't have everything.

You would know everything that was going to be worth the effort before you did it and everything that would not.

Nothing would come as a surprise.

The remarkable, the astonishing, the breathtaking and exquisite moments of life would come as they were foretold and it would be all you could do but to witness them. You would know the single most optimal, and beautiful, and sublime experiences of your life before they were going to happen.

While the universe may well be operating at that level, the facts are that you and I, according to the limits of our perceptions and knowledge, are going to experience life as unpredictable and disordered most of the time.

Both order and chaos then are the result of perspective.

Up and down, light and dark, good and bad. All polarities and oppositions are consequences of positioning and perspective, They are the result of where you stand in the world.

If you perceive imbalance then, and feel impelled to act as a result, you might wish to consider this a creative act. The result of a creative universe operating in accordance with the unique perspective that is you.

NINE

DON'T LET THE BASTARDS GET YOU DOWN

When you open yourself up to life and change, things happen.

When you open yourself up to exploration and discovery, when you begin to question your assumptions, when you commit to knowing and being yourself, when you begin to find out more of who you are and who or what you have the potential to become, when you open up to being truly willing to find out, to create your life and allow life to create you, things happen, and when these things happen, sometimes other people end up getting pissed off.

When you choose to create a life from what you find within you, and allow what you find within you to inform and create life around you, it is more than likely that some of the people you encounter - some of the people whose lives are already entwined with your own - will find your way of living a challenge to their own.

There will be people who don't like what you do because it challenges how they believe people *should* do things.

There will be people who don't like what you do because it challenges what they believe *they* are capable of *doing* or *being* themselves.

There will be people who don't like what you do because they don't find any *meaning* in it, or because they don't *see* any value to it, or because it conflicts with their tastes.

There will be people who don't like what you do because it *intimidates* them.

There will be people who don't like what you do because the connection they have with you is *dependent* upon you not changing, and there will be people who just don't like you for seemingly no reason at all.

Some of these people will share their opinions with you.
Some will want you to change accordingly.
Some can be very persuasive, not least when they are part of a bigger group of people who all share the same ideas.

Some will actively or passively act to see you fail, sometimes this is because it makes them feel more successful, sometimes because it reinforces their reasons for their own sense of failure, sometimes because if they can influence you and in doing so feel like they have more control over their world.

Sometimes they just don't want you to change because they are scared that they will lose you. Sometimes they will be right.

Some people just want to watch the world burn.
Some people are just bastards.

Don't let them get you down.
Don't let the bastards get you down.

When and where you can, remove them from your life.

Where you can't, grow the space where you can reside in your own authenticity more of the time.

Make yourself bigger, stronger, more resilient - both on the outside and within.

Remember what you truly value in life and then be with those things. Trust in them. Trust in yourself.

Do what you love and do what needs to be done: What feels good and what feels right.

Relinquish your fear of failure and your desire for success.

Non attachment, non disinterest.

Remember: Destructive criticism often masks a wound.

And if, after all this, you can find no respite, if after all of this they just kept coming, then relax, stand up straight, and then quietly, under the cover of your breath say the following magic words...

'I appreciate you
and your perspective
but it is not mine.

Now piss off

you stupid bastard.'

... then continue on *your* path.

TEN

BREAK THE RULES

A wise old woman once told me that rules are for fools and the guidance of the wise. I have yet to find an instance when this has not proved to be the case.

There are many rules about how things are made and how things are shared. Some are written in books, others are silent. Some are written with the mind, others on the heart. Some will make sense, some won't.

Discerning which is which will be another step along the path for you.

You may be labelled selfish, irresponsible or even foolhardy in your process of becoming. Only you can ultimately discern if such claims are valid or not.

Is it really selfish to follow the light that guides from within, or is the selfish act the one that asks others to commit to your vision in contravention of their own?

We each have our own path to tread.

By that token, allowing other people the space to follow their paths, and supporting them to do so where you can, is also perhaps something worthy of consideration.

As for breaking the rules, is it ever irresponsible if you are taking responsibility for the consequences of your actions?

Creativity often requires that you break the rules. It just asks that you understand what and why they are before you do.

The same is no less true for everything I have shared in these pages. They are not rules to be followed. If any of it makes sense it will likely be because it resonates with a truth you already knew, or because it wakes a truth you had yet to realise that you knew.

Test it all though.

ELEVEN

MAKE NEW RULES

If you are compelled to be creative, the only success you can be guaranteed of in life is that through creating you will not have to experience the pain and discomfort of not creating.

Let me put that another way.

If you are compelled to create and you do not live creatively then you will experience discomfort. As such the only guarantee that you have in life to not experience the discomfort of not creating, is to create.

Of course, if you are creative in this way, part of the motivation for that creativity can be discomfort too.

Places, things, or processes that are not functioning as well as they could be, or that you find ugly, uninspiring, or that just feel wrong, can be the motivation that inspires the creation of something that *feels* better than what currently is.

As mentioned earlier I suggest that this has something to do with balance; that symmetry and composition, rhythm and pace, all have some sort of sympathetic resonance with the laws of the universe. That you know it when you see it. That you know it when you feel it. That you find yourself drawn to it. It feels comfortable or right in some way, perhaps in nearly every way.

At one level these are qualities that drive creativity. That making things better or more beautiful, or that *feel better* is what a creative life, or living creatively, is really about. As much as it is about improving things or ourselves (whatever that means to you) it is about redressing things that appear, or seem, or feel, out of balance.

At one level, as described in previous chapters, this can be a consciously considered and rational process. We can plan and design things to be better.

It can also be an unconscious engagement too - or, more specifically - it can be guided from a level within us which remains a mystery.

Inspiration, insight and intuition all being evidence of those processes as they are born into consciousness.

Tips of the iceberg so to speak.

At one level you are free to be and do anything that you want. Within the bounds of your conscience and your reason.

Your engagement with your environment, your attitude to it and to yourself, these will show you the limitations of your potential.

Your willingness to discover your potential in life, to remove blocks, to overcome obstacles, to let go of identifications and assumptions, and then to act towards what you can become, whatever that is in the moment, and what ever that might turn out to be, is all that holds you back from becoming who and what you have the potential to be.

The more you meet of this potential and the more you move towards it, the clearer the path can become. While this can require huge energy and commitment at the outset there is a freedom that comes from knowing yourself and feeling the path open up before you. Your choices become clear.

You see your path.

All that is required of you then is that you walk it.

Once you are in that place it is just the effort that is required to move forward.

It works something like this.

By recognising what you love and what needs to be done, what feels good and right to do, by remaining in that place from moment to moment, you reveal yourself to yourself.

You can then start to see and set aside outmoded assumptions, old patterns of behaviour, and things you have identified with in the past that no longer serve you.

You begin to live more and more from a place of who and what you are. The more you do this, the more you learn which bits of your being are consistent and which bits are fleeting.

In this process of becoming you make choices.

Sometimes you will make mistakes.

The mistakes give you feedback.
You learn the lessons they have to offer and move on.
You learn to make better choices as a result.

In this way you learn and transform.

More and more your sense for living in this way grows.

You develop.

You learn that your mind, your gut, and your heart all bear different qualities of knowing.

This intimacy with yourself and with life becomes your teacher.

You learn better to know what feels right and what feels good.

Your intellect comes to serve this, to inform it, but not to control it.

When you are no longer attached to an idea of a self you *need* to create - you relax into being the self you discover yourself to be - and that you are in the process of becoming. That it is not a fixed identity but a process.

Success and failure lose their importance.

Living in the moment of your own authenticity and of your own potential arises as a matter of course.

You recognise that compromising with it only ever leads you away from your path.

You see the process of creation in all things, including you.

You create what you need, what you love, and what feels good, within the limitations that you experience. Limitations that are defined by your experience and your willingness to explore solutions to them, learning those envelopes that can be pushed and those envelopes that cannot.

And you trust in the mystery of all that is beyond you and all that is inside.

Beyond that, from time to time, you will still have to do the dishes. Some rules just can't be broken.

TWELVE

THERE IS NO TWELVE

Sometimes there is no definitive ending,
no final moment of revelation,
no final clarity,
no closure.

Sometimes things end without warning.

Make the most of the path you are on.

There is no other like it. There never will be again.

All the best.

www.CLIVECREATIVE.com